Watch out for fire and fumes!

The bottled gas used for cookers, fridges and heaters is heavier than air and, if there's a leak, it'll lie in the bottom of the boat. There, it only takes a spark to ignite.

Watch out for exhaust fumes building up in the boat. Carbon monoxide is extremely poisonous. Symptoms include headaches, tiredness, sickness and dizziness, and are often mistaken for flu.

- Switch off appliances when you're not using them
- Keep ventilators open and free of obstructions
- If you smell gas or petrol, tell someone straight away

Don't swim!

For your own safety, don't swim in waterways. You could get tangled in weeds, be hit by a passing boat or get drawn into a sluice or weir if you're by a lock. Cold, fast flowing water is dangerous. Don't take the risk.

Don't throw litter overboard!

Please don't throw any waste into the water – even apple cores take a long time to rot. Litter can kill wildlife, and it can cause problems for other boaters by getting tangled in their propellers. There are plenty of bins at marinas, moorings and along the waterway.

Spare a thought for the environment!

Please help to keep the waterways pleasant places for everyone who uses them – and for the wildlife that depends on them.

- Shut gates behind you
- Keep to footpaths
- Don't light fires
- Respect the wildlife

Preface

This booklet resulted from a detailed study of safety information currently available to boaters. The research was carried out by British Waterways and the Environment Agency, with help from the British Marine Federation. As well as introducing the basics of boat-handling, it aims to help people spot risks and avoid accidents.

Feel free to copy it. All we ask is that you don't alter our messages, pictograms or illustrations.

We've tried to make the information in the handbook applicable to inland waterways generally, but local conditions vary, especially on tidal waterways. So always seek local information if you're planning to visit an area that's new to you.

We want the information in the handbook to reach everyone who goes boating on the inland waterways in a powered boat. A pdf version is downloadable from www.waterscape.com/boatershandbook

British Waterways
Customer Service Centre
64 Clarendon Road
Watford WD17 1DA
Tel: 01923 201120   Fax: 01923 201300
enquiries.hq@britishwaterways.co.uk
www.waterscape.com/boating

The Environment Agency
Navigation and Recreation
Rio House, Waterside Drive
Aztec West, Almondsbury
Bristol BS32 4UD
Tel: 08708 506506
enquiries@environment-agency.gov.uk

Association of Inland Navigation Authorities

The Association of Inland Navigation Authorities (AINA) represents almost all inland navigation authorities in the UK. Its purpose is to help with the management, maintenance and development of waterways for economic, environmental and social use.

We're pleased to endorse this important initiative by our two largest members.

The Boater's Handbook

Introduction
Who's in charge?.................3
Before setting off................4

1. **Boat-Handling**
   Setting off 5
   Slowing down and stopping 6
   Steering 6
   Going aground 7
   Mooring 7
   Tying up 8
   Locks 10
   Bridges.........................20
   Tunnels 22
   Winter cruising.................23

2. **Boating Safety**
   Avoiding accidents 24
   Falls...........................24
   Collisions 26
   Crushing........................27
   Operating injuries 28
   Fire, explosion and fumes 29
   Vandalism and aggression 31
   Lock safety 32
   Strong flows, currents and tides ...33
   Man overboard!..................34

3. **Rules of the Road**
   Channel markers 35
   Weirs 35
   Overtaking......................35
   Giving way......................35
   Passing dredgers or works.......36
   Sound signals 36
   Navigation lights 36
   Speed limits 37

4. **Good Boating Behaviour**
   Caring for the environment......37
   Water discharge and oily bilges ...37
   Litter 38
   Wildlife........................38
   Respecting other waterway users .38

5. **Further Information** 39

First published Spring 2002.
Reprinted Spring 2011 with minor revisions.

Welcome to The Boater's Handbook

This handbook gives you all the boating basics – the essential knowledge and techniques you need to make sure you enjoy yourselves and stay safe. Reading it before setting off will help you spot the risks yourself, and help you take simple action to avoid problems. If you do run into difficulties, this understanding will help you get out of trouble quickly and safely.

The Boater's Handbook is designed for newcomers to boating, but we hope it will also be a handy reminder for more experienced boaters.

In part one, we take you through the nitty-gritty of handling your boat. And in part two, you'll find important safety rules to help you keep out of trouble. It's vital stuff. So please – for your own safety – read through carefully.

Part three gives you the basic rules of the road, and part four is all about respecting the environment, the wildlife and other waterways users.

Read this handbook before you set off, and keep it nearby for reference. Of course, you won't become an expert overnight just by reading a book – and it's impossible to cover every aspect of boating, every type of boat and every eventuality.

Short courses in boat handling are an excellent investment. You'll find pointers to these and sources of local information specific to the waterways at the back of the book.

If you're hiring your boat, the operator will give you instructions. Pay close attention – and don't cast off until you feel confident!

Who's in charge?

One of the great things about boating is that everyone can muck in together. But at least one person needs to know the boat-handling basics, to understand the safety guidelines and to know what to do in an emergency.

So, once you've chosen a 'skipper', it'll be his or her job to make sure your crew and passengers have all the information they need to stay safe. It's a good idea to be clear on each crew member's duties.

Good boating takes teamwork. So you need competent crew who know how to handle the boat and how to stop the engine, and who can help with mooring, moving through locks, navigation and so on. As well as knowing the procedures, your crew should be aware of the safety risks in each situation and how to avoid them. It's also a wise precaution to have a stand-in skipper in case you become ill.

Think very carefully before going boating alone as the risks are very much greater.

Passengers who aren't going to be helping with any of the work still need to read and understand the basic safety rules – you'll find a handy safety checklist at the back of this handbook. Please make sure your passengers read it.

These symbols alert you to the most important safety messages. You'll find them at the start of each part of the Boat-Handling section. Read the Boating Safety section thoroughly for full information on the risks and how to avoid them.

Falls	Collisions	Crushing
Operating injuries	Fire, explosion and fumes	Vandalism and aggression

Introduction

Before setting off

Before you set off, take a few simple tips for trouble-free boating.
- Check that your boat is in good condition and meets Boat Safety Scheme standards (see page 40)
- Make sure you and your crew know how to handle the boat – and that you know how to handle it on the waterway you're using
- Get local information from the navigation authority before going onto unfamiliar waterways. On rivers, get information on stream conditions and any tides (see page 39 for links)
- Plan your cruise and allow enough time to complete it without rushing
- It's not a good idea to cruise in the dark or when visibility's bad – if you do, take extra care
- Make sure you've got full tanks of water and fuel
- And remember – alcohol impairs your judgement and makes accidents more likely

Equipment checklist
Make sure you know where to find these things:
- Lifebuoy, lifeline (if supplied), lifejackets or buoyancy aids
- Anchor – for rivers – the rope and chain together should be at least six times as long as the deepest part of the river
- Fire extinguisher and fire blanket
- Emergency shut-offs for battery, gas and fuel
- Bilge pump
- Emergency light
- Mooring ropes – long enough to stretch from your boat to the bollard and back, even when you're in a deep lock
- Mooring stakes and hammer
- Horn
- First aid kit
- Boat pole or hook
- Gangplank
- Windlass (see p12)

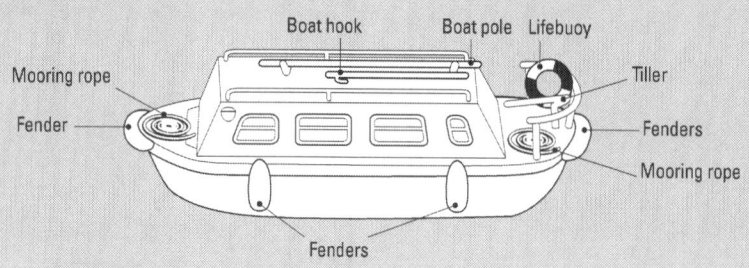

> **Boating jargon**
>
> Front = bow   Right = starboard   Back = stern   Left = port

Setting off

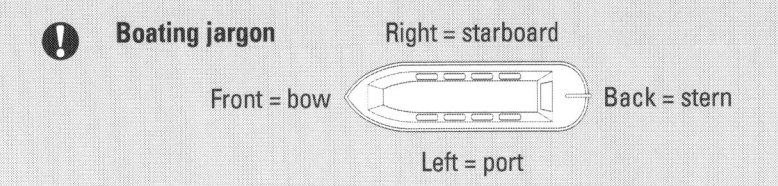

Start the engine, keep it in neutral and allow a few minutes for it to warm up before you move off. Untie the front and back mooring ropes from the bank, but leave them tied to the boat, coiled and ready for use. On rivers, untie the downstream rope first. Make sure your ropes can't trail in the water and get caught in the propeller. Don't forget to stow the mooring stakes and hammer.

Because the boat steers from the back, you can't drive away from the bank as in a car. Check the area is clear of boat traffic then push the boat away from the bank so you can make a clean get away, with your propeller in deep water. In shallow water, push the back of the boat out, then reverse away until there's room to straighten up.

When the boat's straight, go into forward gear and accelerate gently to cruising speed. On all waterways, you drive on the right. In practice, on most canals, you'll keep to the centre of the channel – it's shallow near the edges – unless there's another boat coming towards you.

Always slow down when passing anglers and other boats. Don't let your boat create a breaking wave or a lowering of the water along the bank just ahead of the boat. These are signs that you should throttle back to prevent damage to the bank and disturbance to moored boats. Excessive speed can dislodge mooring pins.

> Boats come in different sizes, shapes and materials – and they all behave differently. Before you set off, spend some time getting to know your boat.

> **Weed or debris around the prop?**
> Remove the weedhatch to check the propeller, but take care. Turn the engine off and take the key out of the ignition. Wear gloves if you can. Always screw the lid back securely.

Slowing down and stopping

Because boats don't have brakes, you need to give yourself plenty of time to stop – especially when travelling downstream on flowing waters. Ease off the throttle, move into neutral and then use short bursts in reverse gear to slow down and come to a final halt. Remember that it's extremely difficult to steer when you're in reverse gear. You may need an occasional forward boost to get better control.

Steering

Steering a boat with a **wheel** is like steering a car, but it's more difficult to judge where your wheel should be for going straight ahead. Get to know the feel of the wheel and the rudder position before you set off.

Using a **tiller** to steer is simple – as long as you remember that pushing to the right will make the boat head left and vice versa. Be patient and plan ahead – the boat will take a few seconds to respond.

Your boat pivots from a point about halfway along its length. That means you need to watch out for the front and the back. If you line up the front only and then try to turn into a narrow gap – a bridge or lock, for example – you risk hitting the side with the back of your boat.

Steering with a tiller

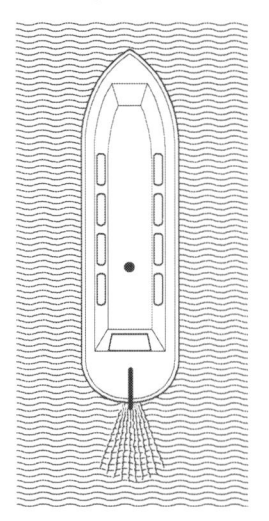

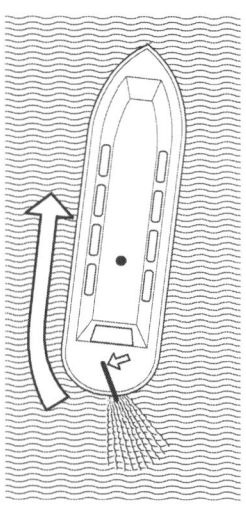

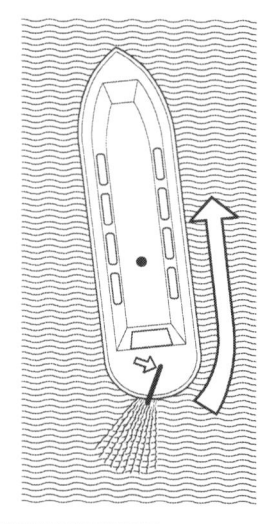

You can't steer unless your boat is in gear. Remember – no gear, no steer

Going aground

Every skipper goes aground at some point – it's not a disaster. Don't try to force your way over the obstacle or you'll find yourself even more stuck. Instead, use reverse gear to back away into deeper water.

If you're firmly stuck, ask some or all of the crew to move to the side of the boat that's still floating (but not to the extent that you'd risk capsizing!). Now use the pole to push off against a solid object or the bed of the waterway – if you put the pole straight down and try to use it as a lever, it'll either break or you'll fall in. And keep the top of the pole away from your face and body, in case it slips suddenly.

✓ Special safety tips
- On a traditional narrowboat, stand inside the hatch so you won't fall off the small back deck – and watch out for the swing of the tiller
- Always be aware of what's happening around you – on the boat, in the water and on the banks
- Don't let passengers stand or sit in the way of the tiller
- Think ahead and make sure you're lined up for bridge and lock entrances well in advance

Mooring

Slow down almost to a stop and carry out all your manoeuvres as slowly as possible.

Stop short of where you want to moor with your boat straight and in deep water. Move forward very slowly, pointing the front of the boat towards the bank, then use reverse to stop the boat just before the front hits the bank. Put the engine into neutral.

On rivers, you should always moor with the front of your boat facing upstream or into a very strong wind. So, if you're heading downstream, you'll need to pass the mooring and turn your boat around. Allow for the fact that the water level may rise or fall by several feet. If it's a tidal river, you should always moor facing the tide – and avoid mooring to the bank overnight.

Your crew should step ashore – not jump. They can either carry the ropes with them – making sure there's plenty of slack and that one end is fixed to the boat – or you can pass them the ropes once they're on land.

Tying up

To keep your boat secure, you need to tie it to the bank with a rope from both the front and the back. On rivers, you should fix your upstream rope first.

Many mooring sites have bollards or rings to tie up to – choose ones a short distance beyond the front and the back of your boat. Run your ropes at about 45° from your boat, loop them back onto the boat and tie securely, but not too tightly.

To stop your boat moving backwards and forwards in flowing water, you can use extra ropes as 'springs' – see example below right.

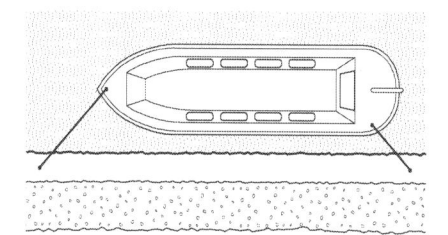

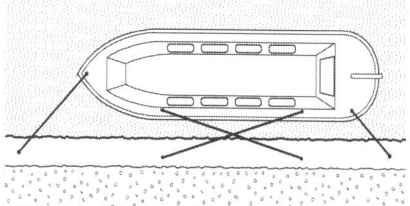

If there aren't any bollards or rings, use your mooring stakes, but check the stability of the bank and watch out for signs of underground pipes or cables before you start hammering. Knock them in to about three-quarters their length and make sure they're firm. Mark them with a piece of light-coloured cloth or a white carrier bag so that other towpath users can see them clearly, and don't tie your ropes across the towpath.

Leave a little slack in your ropes – that's especially important on tidal waterways or rivers. If the ropes are too tight and the water level drops, your boat could be left hanging from the bank.

Remember that your anchor should be used if you need added security or extra help in a strong stream or tide – and you should still use mooring ropes.

Special safety tips

Make sure you know how to use your ropes properly. Keep them coiled, free of knots – and don't drop them in the water, especially near a propeller.

Never be tempted to use your boat's centre line as a mooring rope.

Three useful knots
Locking hitch

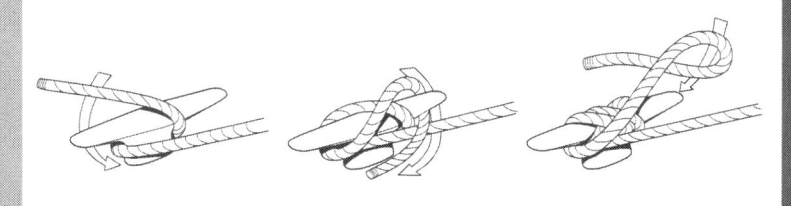

Round turn and two half hitches   Quick release clove hitch

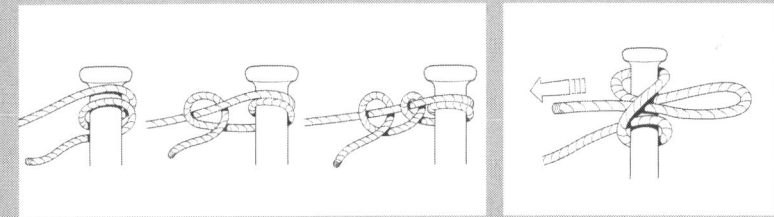

It's well worth learning about these and other knots from specialist books. See page 40.

Can I moor here?
Use signposted visitor moorings wherever possible, and always moor to the towpath if you can. Check that you're not a hazard to other boats or to people using the bank. Moor economically, leaving room for other boats to tie up too. Use authorised sites on rivers. Many riverbanks and the non-towpath side of canals are private property.

Don't moor:
- In lock approaches or in lock flights
- Near swing or lift bridges
- Near weirs
- Near sharp bends
- By blind spots
- In or opposite turning points
- At junctions
- To the bank on a tidal river – you might find yourself hanging from the ropes when the tide goes out!
- In stretches marked out for an angling match
- And try to stay 50 feet (15m) away from established angling spots

Locks

There's no mystery to using locks – just a series of step-by-step tasks. Know the procedure, take your time and you'll be on your way with no problem.

A lock is simply a chamber with gates at either end. By emptying or filling that chamber with water, your boat can move up or down onto a new section of the waterway.

Although there are many different kinds of locks, they all work on a similar principle. With the lock gates closed, you open sluices (the paddles) to let the water in or out. When the water level under your boat is the same as the level you're moving to, you simply move in or out of the lock.

Some locks you operate yourself and others are operated by lock-keepers. Check your particular waterway for details. Always obey specific lock instructions and local information.

Special safety tips
- Take your time – and keep an eye out for problems
- Enter and leave slowly so bumps are less likely to cause damage
- Always have a competent person on board while the boat's in the lock
- Keep your boat well away from the gates and cills.
- Boats tend to bang about when water flows in and out of a lock – stay alert
- When using fenders, make sure they don't get caught up on the lockside or gates
- Watch out for slippery surfaces when you're pushing the gates open
- Work out some clear signals so that the crew and skipper can communicate quickly – a signal that means "close all the paddles", for example
- Wait for the boat already in the lock to leave before you start opening or closing paddles. Ask first before helping other boaters to complete the lock operation.
- Watch out for unprotected drops around the lockside, especially when opening gates.

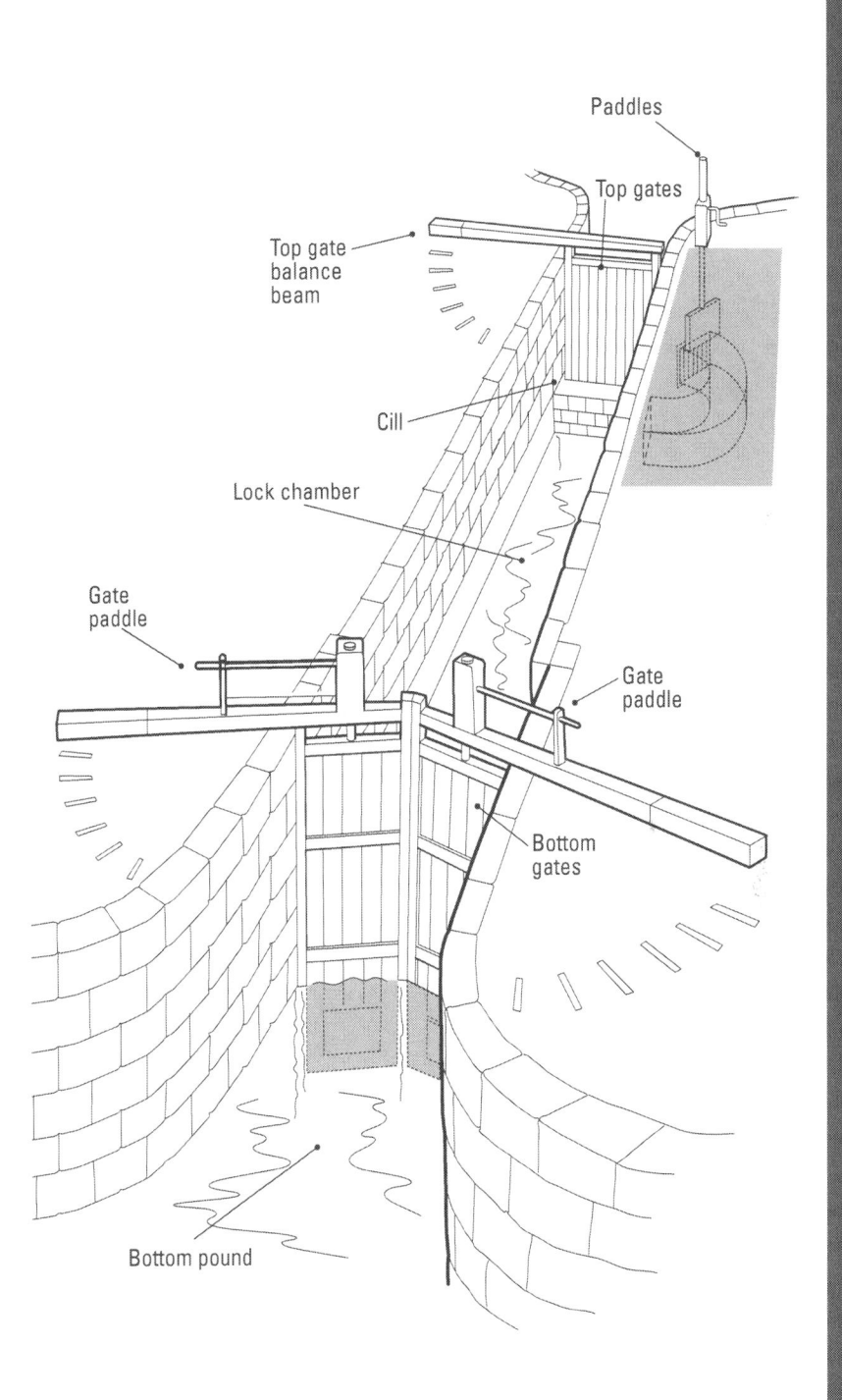

Paddles
Top gates
Top gate balance beam
Cill
Lock chamber
Gate paddle
Gate paddle
Bottom gates
Bottom pound

Boat-Handling

(11)

Working the paddle gear

Upstream paddles fill the lock. Downstream ones empty it. Paddle gear can be either hydraulic or rack and pinion. On the rack and pinion type, remember to engage the safety catch before winding up the paddles. This stops the gears from slipping down. When you've finished winding the paddles up, check the safety catch is in position and then take off your windlass.

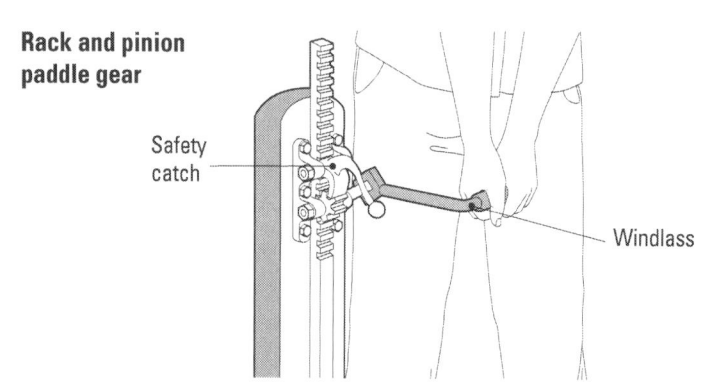

Rack and pinion paddle gear

Safety catch

Windlass

With one crew member at the helm and one at the paddles, you wind the paddle gear up and down using a windlass or lock key. You should always wind them bit-by-bit – and keep an eye on the effect of the moving water on your boat.

To close the paddle, take the weight on your windlass, then lift off the safety catch and wind the paddle down – if you let it drop, the spinning windlass could injure you.

Special safety tips
- A flying windlass is lethal! To avoid an accidental launch:
  - Keep a firm grip and don't let go
  - Only use a windlass that fits the spindle snugly
  - Make sure the windlass is slotted onto the spindle fully
  - Always use the safety catch when winding paddles up
  - Never leave the windlass on the spindle unattended

- Keep fingers, hair and clothing away from the gears.

Navigating unmanned locks

Going uphill

As you approach the lock, send one of your crew to check whether it's full of water or empty. If it's empty, they can open the gates and you can steer straight in.

If it's full, moor up below the lock, far enough away to avoid the currents while the lock is emptying. Empty the lock by slowly raising the paddles. Open the gates and steer in.

Close the gates and the paddles (or check that these are already down if the lock was ready for you).

If there are ground paddles by the top gate, open these first. Wait until the lock is half full before opening the gate paddles. If there are only gate paddles, open them **very** slowly, especially if the paddles are above the low water level. (See warning picture overleaf).

Keep your boat steady using front and back ropes looped round the bollards – take an extra turn around the bollard to stop the boat pulling you, but don't tie up. Take a look at Floating Freely? on page 16.

When it's full, open the gates and take your boat out. Lower the paddles – and close the gates behind you unless a boat coming towards you wants to use the lock.

If the gates don't open or close easily, wait till the water level's absolutely equal. If there's still a problem, close the gates and paddles, check for trapped debris and remove it with your boat-hook.

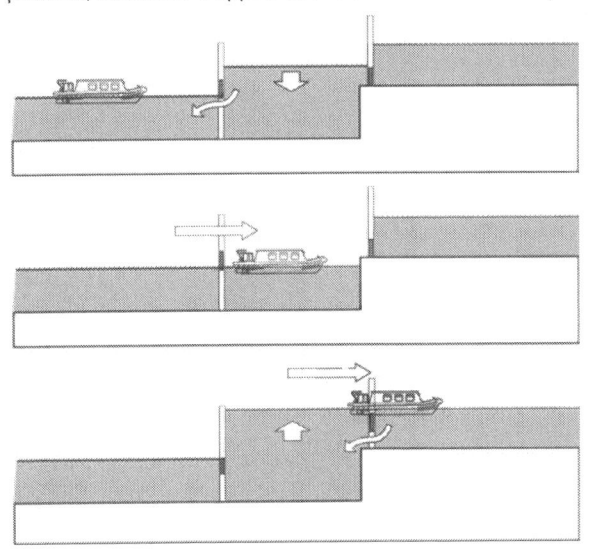

Most locks also have ground paddles alongside the gates.
In this sort of lock, you must use the ground paddles first to partly fill the lock. Wait till the gate paddles are under water before you open them, or you will swamp your boat. To stop your boat from banging about, loop ropes round the lockside bollards before you start to fill the lock.

This is what can happen if you open the gate paddles too soon

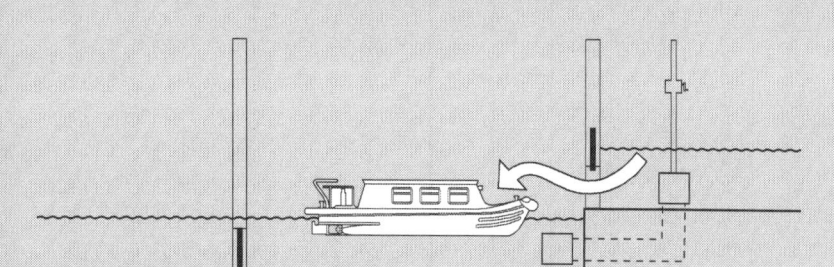

Going downhill
If the lock's already full, open the gates and steer straight in. If it's not, check that the far gates and paddles are closed and then fill the lock by opening the paddles at the end nearest to the boat. When the lock's full, open the gate and steer in. Close the gates and lower the paddles.

Open the paddles in front to empty the lock, using your engine or ropes to keep the boat as still as possible. Keep the back of your boat well forward of the cill below the top gates – cills stick out by up to 5ft (1.5m) and you can only see them as the lock empties. Most locks have markers to show you the approximate position of the cill.

When the water levels are equal, open the bottom gates and take the boat out. Close the gates and lower the paddles before you move on, unless a boat coming from the opposite direction wants to use the lock.

Sharing a lock – saving water

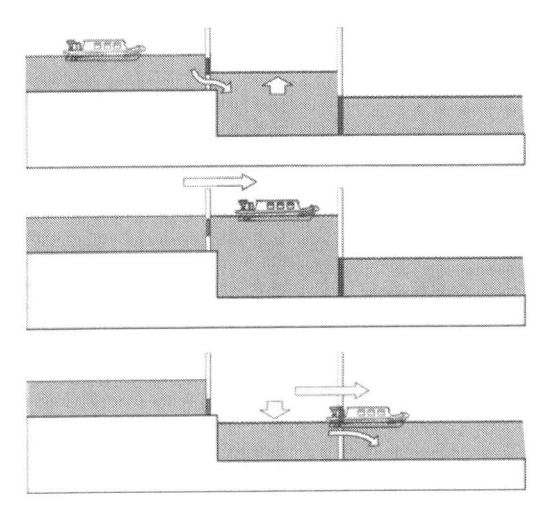

Always share a lock if you can. And, if the lock's set against you, check for boats coming from the other direction. The lock will be ready for them to use and it'll save unnecessary emptying and filling.

It's sometimes possible to get two short boats end-to-end in a narrow lock, but check that you both have enough room to avoid the cill and gates. The heavier boat should always go in first, so that the water flow doesn't pull it into the lighter boat.

In broad locks, boats should be kept to the side with ropes looped round the bollards. Open the two paddles equal amounts, at the same time where possible – and slowly.

Some lock walls taper from top to bottom so if you're travelling side by side with another boat, make sure there's plenty of room between you.

Special safety tips

- If you use ropes to keep the boat steady in the lock, don't try to take the full strain of the boat directly with the rope – wind it once around the bollard...
- and take special care not to let your fingers get between the rope and the bollard.

Floating freely?
As the water level rises or falls, keep a continual check on your boat.
- **Is the side of your boat caught against the lock wall?** (going either upstream or downstream) Refill the lock and check for damage
- **If you're sharing the lock with another boat, is there a safe distance between you?** (going either upstream or downstream)
  Use ropes looped round the bollards to keep you in position
- **Is the front of your boat caught on the top gate?** (going upstream)
  Close the top gate paddles to stop the lock filling. Open the bottom gate paddles to allow the water level to fall
- **Is your rudder caught on the cill?** (going downstream)
  Close the bottom gate paddles to stop the water falling further. Slowly open the top gate paddles to refill the lock. Check for damage
- **Are your ropes snarled or too tight to let your boat move down freely?** (going downstream) Slacken them off if you can. If not, refill the lock

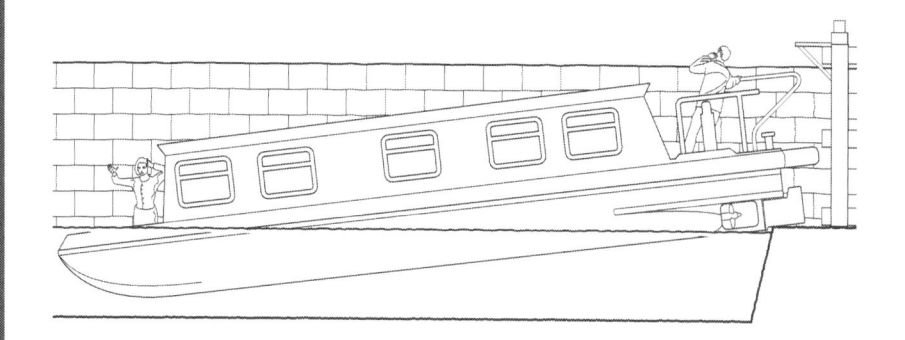

If someone falls into the lock, act quickly. If there's no lock-keeper to take charge:
- Close all paddles – while water is flowing, it entraps air which reduces buoyancy
- Throw a lifeline or lifebuoy
- Stop the engine and keep the boat still
- If there's no ladder – or the person can't climb – you may need to fill the lock SLOWLY to bring them up to your level. Or, if the lock is almost empty, <u>slowly</u> lower the water level, open the gate and draw the person to safety using the lifeline
- NEVER jump into the water yourself to rescue someone who has fallen in

Manned locks

Some waterways have manned locks, operated by a lock-keeper. Always follow the lock-keeper's instructions. You can operate some of these yourself out-of-hours, but check local information for details. On some waterways – the Thames, for example – you must switch your engine off in the lock, and use ropes to control your boat.

If the lock has traffic light signals, amber usually means it is on user-operation and you should proceed with care. Check local information.

Guillotine locks

You'll find guillotine locks on the East Anglian waterways. They have steel or wooden pointing gates – also known as mitre doors – at one end, and vertical guillotine gates at the other end. Some are electrically-operated and others are wound up and down by hand.

Use your fenders to stop your boat getting caught on the safety chains that run alongside the lock.

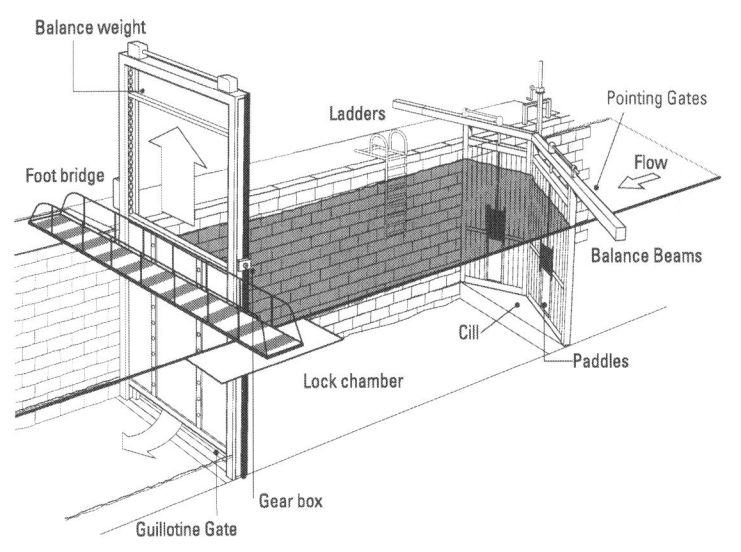

Diagram labels: Balance weight, Ladders, Pointing Gates, Foot bridge, Flow, Balance Beams, Cill, Paddles, Lock chamber, Gear box, Guillotine Gate

Gates open?

Go into the lock slowly and moor up. Make sure the guillotine gate, pointing gates and paddles (if there are any) are closed.

Depending on which way you're going, open the paddles in the pointing doors or lift the guillotine gate a few centimetres **slowly**. If the water flows in or out of the lock too quickly, close the gate and start again.

The crew in charge of the mooring lines should keep the ropes taut as water levels change.

When the water levels are equal, open the pointing doors or guillotine gate fully – depending on which way you're headed.

Close the paddles in the doors before you leave.

Gates closed?

Moor up at the landing stage and check that all doors, gates and paddles are closed.

Fill the lock **slowly**. When the levels are equal, open the doors or gate fully, steer into the lock and follow the procedure above.

When you've finished using the lock, always leave the pointing doors closed and the vertical gate raised, secured and locked, unless directed otherwise.

Staircase locks

Sometimes, you'll find two, three, four or even five locks joined in a staircase. That means the bottom gates of one lock are also the top gates of the next, and water from one lock fills the lock below. Usually you need to prepare all the locks before you start through the staircase.

Never empty a lock unless the one below it is already empty.
But bear in mind that locks should never be completely empty – the lowest water level should still be deep enough to float your boat. Some staircase locks have markers to show you the level. Once you've prepared the locks, make sure all the paddles are fully closed.

If the water level isn't right, you could get stuck on the cill between the locks. If you do, just make sure the paddles below the boat are closed and slowly let the water into the lock from the lock above using the ground paddles only.

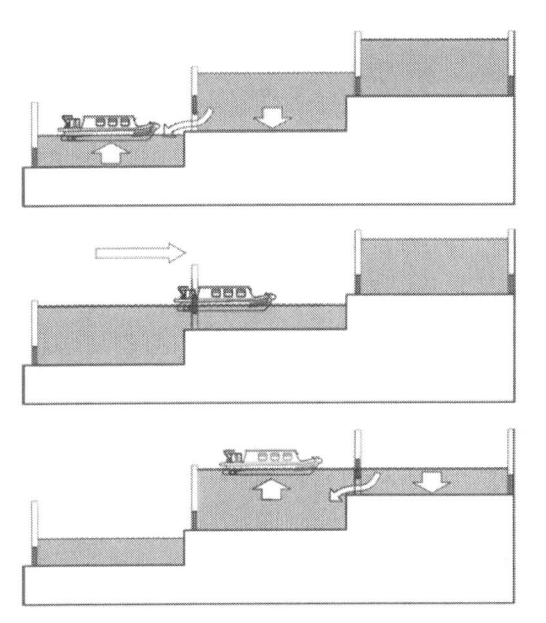

Going uphill

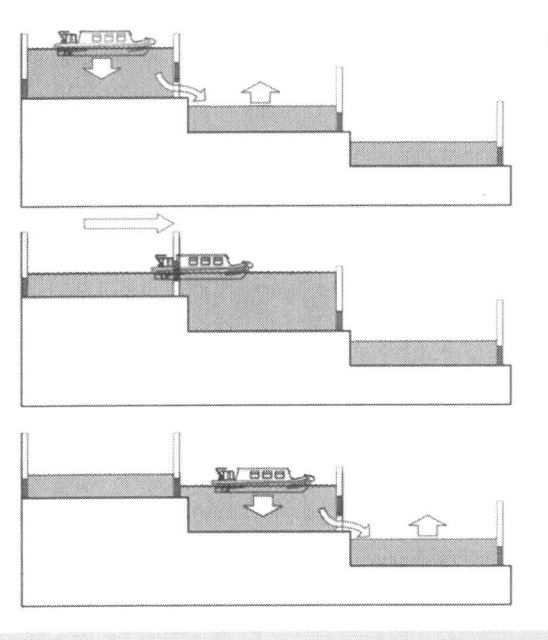

Going downhill

> **Stumped by the staircase?**
> Usually if you're going uphill, the bottom lock should be empty and the rest full. If you're going downhill, the top lock should be full and the others empty. But this doesn't always apply (for example, at Foxton and Watford Flights) so do check local instructions, on a notice board or in your guidebook.

Bridges

You'll come across a whole range of bridges on your travels. Some are fixed and some need to be moved out of the way to let your boat pass. Get information on what sorts of bridge to expect on your journey from the navigation authority or by reading a local waterway guide.

Remember that many bridges have low headroom. Weather conditions upstream have an effect on river water levels – adequate clearance today might disappear tomorrow if water levels rise.

Bridges can be narrow too, which means river water tends to speed up as you get nearer. This can draw your boat towards the bridge, so stay alert. Boats travelling downstream on rivers have the right of way at bridges and narrows.

Swing and lift bridges

Well before you reach the bridge, land your crew with the windlass or key.

If it's a traffic bridge, check that the road's clear and close the warning barriers if there are any. Don't forget to open the barriers once the bridge is back in place.

Manual swing bridges

Let your crew off well before the bridge – it's easier then to get the boat lined up correctly. Unhook the retaining chain and give the bridge a good – but controlled – shove. You might need to slow the swing down to stop the bridge bouncing back across the canal when it hits the buffer stop.

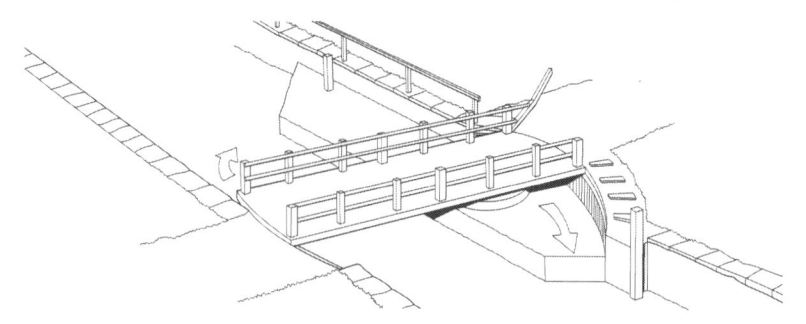

When the boat's through, push the bridge firmly into place and put the retaining chain or lock back on.

Manual lift bridges

Pull the chain hanging from the balance arm. When the bridge is open, unless it's obvious that there's a mechanism to stop the bridge from lowering by itself, sit an adult on the arm to keep it raised until the boat's clear.

Gently lower the bridge by the chain, taking care not to let it drop.

Mechanised bridges

Mechanised bridges are either opened using the windlass, or are powered and need a navigation authority facilities key. Always follow the instructions.

With some swing and lift bridges, you can't move the traffic barriers until you've unlocked the control box. And you can't move the barriers back again until the bridge is back in its original position.

Windlass-operated bridges need to be unlocked first, but you must make sure you lock them again before cars are allowed back over.

Some modern bridges use wedges to stop them bouncing when cars drive over. You should find instructions at the bridge on how to release them. Always make sure they're back in place, though, or traffic will damage the bridge mechanism.

Bridge trouble?
If a bridge breaks down, don't try to force it. Call the local navigation office for help. There should be a phone number on the bridge instructions. If not, call the local navigation authority office or Helpline (see page 39).

Safety tips
- Don't try to take your boat through until the bridge is fully open and secure (they can stick at the wrong moment)
- Take care with clearance under lift and fixed bridges and stay in the centre of the channel
- Keep everyone off the roof and within the profile of the boat
- Watch out for slippery surfaces when you're pushing swing bridges
- Use strong, fit crew to operate moving bridges

Tunnels

Tunnels can be narrow with only room for one-way traffic, or they can be wide enough for two boats to pass. Check for instructions, entry times or traffic lights at the tunnel entrance.

If it's a one-way tunnel, make sure there's no boat inside. If you have to wait your turn, stay well clear of the entrance.

Switch on your headlight and some interior lights. Some stern lighting will help a following boat to see you, but if it's a single bright spot or rear navigation light, it might be confused with a headlight by the helmsman of a following boat.

It can be damp in there, so put on your waterproofs and have a waterproof torch to hand.

As you go in, sound one long blast on your horn. Now steer by looking at one side of the tunnel only and keep to a moderate speed. Move the tiller or wheel as little as possible – it's a common illusion to feel the boat's being pulled to the side. Watch out for the changing profile, though – tunnels are rarely straight.

Keep at least two minutes (at normal cruising speed) or about **500ft (160m)** away from any boat in front of you. If it's two-way traffic, keep a look-out for oncoming boats and pass slowly on the right.

✓ **Special safety tips**
- Keep your crew and passengers inside the profile of the boat in tunnels and aqueducts
- Make sure you have enough fuel to get you through
- If you break down in a tunnel, switch off the engine
- Don't smoke or use cookers and heaters. Turn off the gas except pilot lights
- Help the steerer by stopping inside lights from shining on the back of the boat

Winter cruising

Unless your journey is really necessary, don't cruise through ice. Even thin breaking ice can puncture timber and fibreglass hulls. Thicker ice can also damage steel hulls of boats that you pass, or your own.

Watch your footing at all times

Don't take risks – wear a life jacket

Wear gloves to stop your hands sticking to icy surfaces such as bridge arms and paddle handles

Wrap up warm – good insulation will help prevent hypothermia.

Avoiding accidents

Now we've shown you the safe way to do all the main boating things, we'd like to say a bit more about accidents.

Tranquil waterways, beautiful scenery, fresh air. Boating on our canals and rivers is a real pleasure – and, most of the time, there's no safer way to travel.

Accidents and injuries are rare, but every year a few people do get hurt – usually through inexperience or not paying attention. If you do have an accident or near-miss, you should report it to the local waterway office or member of staff on the bank. Your report could help to save others.

By looking at the accidents people have had on boats over the past few years, we've found that they fit into a relatively small number of categories – see the symbols at the front of the book. This part of the booklet tells you about these so that you can avoid the same misfortune.

Don't let small children move around the boat unsupervised. Always know where they are.

Falls

Wherever you are – home, work or on a waterway – the most common accidents are slips, trips and falls. But when you fall off a boat or from the waterside, those accidents can be more serious.

Apart from the risk of drowning, you could be dragged or fall into a moving propeller. You could hit your head, or be crushed between your boat and another object. There's also a slight risk of infection from the water itself.

Boats and watersides are littered with bollards, rings, ropes and holes. Surfaces can be uneven or slippery, particularly in wet or icy weather or early morning dew. So you need to keep your eyes open – and slow down.

Many falls happen during mooring – simply because people aren't sure of the procedure.

There are unprotected drops at locksides. Watch out especially when operating lock gates.

What causes falls?
- Trips over ropes, mooring stakes and so on – especially when left untidy
- Walking on narrow decks on boats that tend to rock
- Jumping off or stepping off in a dangerous place
- Slipping on a wet deck
- Moving about the boat or waterside at night
- Too much to drink

Safety essentials
- Watch out for collisions – and if you <u>are</u> going to bump, warn your crew and passengers
- Always use the grab rail
- Keep your boat tidy
- Don't jump off the boat when mooring
- Wear non-slip deck-shoes
- Take extra care on towpaths at night. Always use a torch

Don't leave the helm when the engine's running. If someone falls into the water, they could be injured by the moving propeller. And don't leave the keys in the ignition unattended. Never run the propeller when the boat's moored up.

Should I wear a lifejacket?
Children, non-swimmers and lone boaters should wear lifejackets whenever they're on deck. And that applies to everyone if you're negotiating tidal waters, strong streams or currents or if the decks are slippery and whenever the water is likely to be cold.
Of course, it's always safer to wear a lifejacket or buoyancy garment – but check conditions and use your judgement.

True stories
Eyes in the back of your head?
Eleven-year-old Sam was lucky to escape with a broken arm when he fell onto the deck of a boat as it passed through a lock.
While the rest of his family – relatively experienced holiday boaters – were busy with the 60ft narrowboat, Sam ran along the lockside, tripped over a bollard and fell over the edge. Luckily, the lock-keeper was on hand to rescue him.

Collisions

Collisions – with other boats, banks, bridges or other structures – are another common cause of injury. The impact can lead to falls, both onto the deck and into the water. And for people working in the galley, there's a risk of scalds or burns.

What causes collisions?
- Lack of boat-handling skill or experience
- Taking your eyes off the waterway
- Cruising too fast

Safety essentials
- Make sure you know the size of your boat and the dimensions of the waterway you're cruising on
- Check headroom for bridges. Remember bridge shapes vary and water levels rise
- Watch out for cross-winds
- Be ready for strong flows at locks, weirs and places where water is taken in or out of the waterway
- Give a long blast with the horn as you approach blind bridges, bends and junctions
- Look out for canoes and dinghies
- Watch out for floating tree trunks and other debris
- Learn the Rules of the Road

True stories
Blast it!
Neither skipper sounded the warning when a small cruiser and a family on a first-time boating holiday met at a blind bend.
The collision sent a sunbather flying from the deck of the hire boat. The quick-thinking helmsman stopped the propellers just in time, and the girl was rescued unharmed. An elderly woman on the cruiser wasn't so lucky – she'd been making tea in the galley and was badly scalded.

Waterborne diseases, including Weil's Disease (leptospirosis), are extremely rare, but it's sensible to take a few precautions.
If you've got any cuts or scratches, keep them covered. If you fall in, take a shower and treat cuts with antiseptic and a sterile dressing. Wash wet clothing before you wear it again.
If you develop flu-like symptoms within two weeks, see your doctor and mention that you fell in the water. Not all doctors will know to look for signs of Weil's Disease, so do suggest it as a possibility.

Crushing

If your boat collides with something else, you don't want to be in the way. Don't put yourself between the boat and a bank, tunnel or bridge, or you could end up with crushed fingers or legs – or even more serious body injuries.

What causes injuries?
- Using your hands or feet to stop a collision or fend off
- Not appreciating the momentum or the size of your boat

Safety essentials
- Keep your body out of the way
- Keep within the boat – that means not having your legs dangling over the side, your hands over the edge or your head out of the side hatch
- Keep off the roof when underway
- Don't fend off with your arms, legs or a boat pole – let the fender take the impact
- Make sure anyone in the front cockpit is on the look-out for possible collisions

True stories
Helping hand – broken ankle
A couple, invited along for a canal cruise by their neighbours, were eager to help. So, approaching a mooring, the husband leapt to the front of the boat with the mooring rope. Seeing the boat was about to hit the bank, he instinctively stuck out a foot to fend off. His pleasure trip ended with a broken ankle, crushed between the boat and the bank.

Operating injuries

Boating can involve a lot of physical exercise. Some of the work is heavy and you'll also be using unfamiliar techniques and tools. Together, the two things can add up to strained backs and muscles, cuts or worse.

What causes operating injuries?
- Overstretching yourself
- Using tools or equipment incorrectly
- Not paying attention to the job in hand

Safety essentials
- Take things easy. Don't strain. Share the work
- Let the fittest operate locks and bridges
- Make sure you know how to use equipment properly
- Watch out for worn paddle gear
- Only use a boat-hook or pole when the boat's still
- Keep fingers clear of ropes – sudden tension in the rope can trap fingers
- Don't wrap ropes around any part of your body
- Don't use ropes to stop the boat – use the engine
- Don't push off from the side of another boat with your pole. It could slip on the smooth surface.

True stories
Tools that bite back
Take a lesson from this hire boat crew, coming across their first lock. One of the helpers left the windlass on the spindle and then let go. The ratchet slipped and spun the handle round, breaking her nose and teeth.

Rope tricks
Crushed fingers and rope burns were the painful end to a holiday for this crew member. While holding the mooring rope around a bollard, a sudden tug from the boat pulled the rope – and his fingers – into the bollard. His fingers were trapped until the skipper brought the boat further in and the rope slackened off.

Fire, explosion and fumes

Boat fires and explosions are extremely rare – probably because most people take the same sensible precautions as they do at home. But there are some specific risks to be aware of.

The bottled gas used for cookers, fridges and heaters is heavier than air and, if there's a leak, it'll build up in the bottom of the boat. A small spark will ignite this gas.

Petrol vapour is also heavier than air and highly flammable. If there's a strong smell of gas or petrol, follow the drill on the next page.

And lastly, you need to watch out for fumes from cookers, cabin heaters and water heaters or from engine exhaust building up in the boat. Carbon monoxide poisoning is extremely dangerous - early signs include headaches, tiredness, sickness and dizziness, and other flu-like symptoms. Anyone affected should see a doctor straightaway.

What causes injuries from fire, explosion or fumes?
- Dangerous misuse of equipment or the failure of some parts of the fuel, gas or electrical system
- Unsafe handling or stowage of petrol and gas containers. These must not be kept in cabins or engine spaces
- Poor ventilation, leaking flues and a build-up of petrol engine exhaust fumes

Safety essentials
- Boat appliances and their fuel systems need regular checks and professional servicing
- Learn how to refuel safely
- Never store gas containers in the cabin, even empty ones (and not even for a short time)
- Ensure all electrical circuits are protected by appropriate fuses or circuit breakers
- Make a *fire action plan* with your crew to help your escape if the worst happens. Make sure you know where your fire extinguishers are, and how to use them
- Keep ventilators open and free of obstructions
- If you're leaving a solid fuel burner alight overnight, open a window for extra ventilation

Safe re-fuelling of petrol engines and generators
- Stop the engine, switch off ignition systems
- Put out all naked flames including pilot lights
- Evacuate the boat if possible

(Continued Overleaf)

- Vapour will travel, so protect the boat by closing doors and hatches etc
- Never refuel in a lock or next to another boat
- Refuel outboard tanks and generator tanks ashore, well away from the boat
- Wipe up any spillage immediately and replace the cap on the can, securely

True stories
Breathe easy! A sunny autumn weekend? Perfect weather for a day's cruising. But when the night turned chilly, this boating couple blocked off the draughty ventilators and lit the gas central heating. When their friends came back from the pub, they found the couple unconscious from carbon monoxide poisoning. Had they stayed for a last drink, the result would have been far worse than severe headaches.

Hey! I can smell gas (or petrol)!
Close the shut-off valve and open windows, hatches or doors to ventilate the area as much as possible. Turn the engine off, and put out naked flames, cookers, pilot lights and cigarettes. Evacuate the boat if possible.

Don't switch anything electrical on or off, including lights and the bilge pump, until you're sure the gas/petrol has dispersed.
Find the problem and get it put right before you turn the gas on again.

Fire! Act quickly – fire spreads rapidly! Put your *fire action plan* into practice! Alert everyone on board to move to a safe location and evacuate if possible. Call the fire service if you can. Use a fire blanket on pan fires, and fire extinguisher on other fires. They can help you escape or to fight a small fire, if you feel competent. Keep these maintained in good condition and ready for use at any time.

If the fire's in the engine space, **don't** open the main access – the air will only feed the fire. Some boats have a fixed fire extinguisher in the engine space. It may be automatic or may have a manual control outside the compartment. Failing this, you might be able to discharge a fire extinguisher through a small opening in the engine access, or air inlet.

If someone's clothes are alight, quickly lie them face down so that the flames rise away from their face. Smother the flames with a blanket or wet jacket, laid away from their face. Call the emergency services.

Further reading Boat Safety Scheme (BSS) has a range of 'Go boating – Stay safe!' leaflets, A silent threat – Carbon Monoxide; Safe use of LPG – Safe use of petrol – Avoiding fire afloat; Fire action plans and ways of preventing a fire are explained in the BSS 'Avoiding fire afloat' leaflet. The BSS Essential Guide is available to view, download or order on www.boatsafetyscheme.com

Vandalism and aggression

There's little that's more peaceful than cruising a stretch of quiet waterway. But in a very few urban areas, things aren't as laid-back as they should be. Some gangs of youths think of the waterway as their own. Keep an eye out for trouble-makers.

The main problems to watch for are missiles being thrown from banks or bridges, and theft.

How to avoid problems
- Watch out for vandals throwing missiles at tunnel entrances and exits, dropping objects from bridges, or jumping into the water
- Keep a low profile and avoid confrontation
- Don't moor where there could be a risk
- Know your location in case you need to call for help
- Have a cheap camera and a mobile phone to hand
- Keep valuables out of sight

If things get difficult
- Call the police
- Keep a safe distance away if you can
- Stay calm. Do not antagonise the aggressors
- Speak clearly and firmly. Don't raise your voice or argue
- Maintain eye contact and use positive responses
- Be understanding but don't get involved in arguments

True stories
Thugs with too much bottle
A gang of teenagers, fooling around on the canal towpath, asked a passing boater to give them a ride. When the skipper turned them down, they turned nasty. Ten minutes later, they were back – this time waiting on a bridge, armed with bricks and bottles. The crafty boater scared them off by taking photos of them from a safe distance.

Lock safety

Though boating accidents are few and far between, many of them happen in locks.

Moving through a lock is perhaps the trickiest part of boating. There's a lot to think about at once and a whole series of tasks to carry out.

Practically all the safety tips we've come across so far apply here. But you also need to be extra alert. If your boat gets caught up, it could come crashing down into the lock.

There's more guidance on how to use locks on pages 10 to 19.

What causes accidents in locks?
- Not paying attention
- Rushing the procedures

Safety essentials
- Make sure the boat's level and free. It should be away from the cill, not caught on a gate or projection and the ropes should be able to run freely
- Use the paddles (sluices) gradually
- Make sure that each member of the crew sticks to their allotted task - accidents happen when crew wander off, especially with a big crew
- Adult crew must be in charge of the lock
- Watch out for 'helpful' bystanders – their mistakes could land you in trouble
- Always have a steerer on the boat in locks

True stories
Stay alert – stay afloat
They were experienced hirers, well-used to using locks, but while the crew opened the paddles to let out the water, the helmsman went inside the boat to put the kettle on.

The front of the boat caught on the lock gate and the back of the boat continued to float down – the crew didn't notice until it was too late. As the water level dropped, the front of the boat crashed down, flooded and sank. Though badly shocked, the helmsman wasn't injured. The canal, though, had to be closed and a crane hired to raise the boat.

Fast-flowing water

Most canals are calm and smooth-flowing, but rivers can catch you out with strong streams, currents or, in some cases tides. Handling a boat in fast-flowing water takes special skill and good judgement. What's more, the usual risks are magnified – a current makes collisions more likely, for example, and can make it harder to recover a person overboard.

What causes accidents?
- Inexperience
- Taking on too much of a challenge

Safety essentials
- Don't cruise in strong stream conditions – tie up securely, watch for changes in water level and adjust your mooring ropes as necessary
- Make sure your boat has enough power to cope with the strength of the stream or tide
- Have a good anchor and chain ready for use
- Steer clear of weirs
- Boating with an experienced skipper is the best way to gain experience
- Look out for big commercial boats and prepare to give way

True stories
Ignoring warning leads to tragedy
There'd been several days of heavy rain and the river level was rising, but this boater – out in his own fibreglass cruiser with his girlfriend – ignored the strong stream warning signs. Instead of tying up, he tried to reach a canal and his boat was swept sideways down the river. As it wedged against a bridge, his girlfriend fell overboard and was swept away.

If you're venturing onto or leaving a strong stream or tidal waters, make sure you're prepared – get information on unfamiliar waterways, take advice and obey warning signs.

Man overboard!

Before you do anything else, take a breath and think. Don't panic, don't jump in – and don't let others jump in. The water is very cold even in summer. Keep sight of the person in the water at all times.

On narrow canals and slow, shallow rivers

Turn your engine off. **Don't** reverse the boat – the person in the water could be dragged into the propeller.

Throw a line or a lifebelt and tell them to try to stand up – if it's a canal they might be able to walk out.

Steer the boat slowly to the bank and get one of your passengers to help the person to shore.

On wider or deeper waterways

Throw a lifebuoy or line and steer your boat carefully to approach the person in the water. Keep a constant watch to ensure your propeller is well away from them. Stop the propeller immediately by selecting neutral gear if there's a risk of them getting close to it.

Pull them to the side of the boat and help them aboard with a ladder, rope or pole.

Be prepared

Make sure everyone on the boat knows the drill – and knows where to find the lifeline or lifebelt. In case it's the skipper who falls overboard, the crew should also know how to stop the propeller and steer the boat.

Practice the drill. It's better to learn it **before** an accident happens.

Never swim in waterways. You could:
- Get tangled in weeds
- Be hit by a passing boat
- Get drawn into a sluice or weir
- Catch a waterborne disease

Cold, fast-flowing water is dangerous. Don't take the risk!

Channel markers

If there's a channel you should stick to it – it'll usually be marked by buoys or by red cans and green cones. If you're heading downstream, keep the red cans to your right and the green cones to your left. If you're going upstream, the red markers should be on your left and the green on your right.

Weirs

Straying out of the channel can be very dangerous – especially if you find yourself near a weir. Watch out for the warning signs.

Overtaking

You will rarely need to overtake on canals and narrow rivers. In fact, there isn't usually enough space to overtake safely.

If you do have to overtake, make sure the other skipper knows what you're intending to do well before you start to manoeuvre. They need time to slow down and to tell you on which side to overtake – usually the left. If you're the one overtaking, it's your responsibility to stay clear of the other boat.

Go as slowly as possible to avoid the two boats being drawn together.

Giving way

If you're approaching a bridge or narrow section, slow down. If a boat coming in the opposite direction is closer to the bridge, wave them through and keep right until they're well clear. If someone's waved you through, signal your acknowledgement.

On rivers, the boat coming downstream has right of way.

Rules of the Road

Passing dredgers or works

Pass on the side that's showing the green or white light or shape – not the side showing red. On canals, though, you may see both sides marked with red during the day – follow the instructions given by the works crew.

Sound signals

1 blast = going to the right
2 blasts = going to the left
3 blasts = I'm trying to stop or go backwards
4 blasts – pause – 1 blast = turning round to the right
4 blasts – pause – 2 blasts = turning round to the left
1 long blast + 2 short blasts = I can't manoeuvre
1 extra long blast = warning at tunnels, blind bends and junctions

Navigation lights

It's best not to cruise in the dark. If you do, you must get information from the navigation authority in charge of your waterway. The rules governing navigation lights are quite complex. As a guide, at night and in poor visibility, boats usually show:

White lights – front and back
Green light – right side
Red light – left side
As a result, if you see:
- A white light above a red one, it's likely to be a boat crossing from your right to the left side
- White above green is likely to be a boat crossing left to right
- White above green and red means the boat is coming towards you
- Unpowered boats may show a single all-round white light

> **Cruising at night can be dangerous. Moor up before it gets dark and avoid using locks at night. Cruising after dark is not permitted by hire boat companies.**

Speed limits

The maximum speed on narrow canals is 4mph. But if you're making waves or your wash is hitting the bank, you're going too fast – slow down. On rivers and broad canals, check local information before you set out and watch for speed limit signs en route.

Don't forget that river currents can increase and decrease the speed of your boat.

Keep your speed down when you're approaching bridges, locks, bends or junctions, and when passing other boats or anglers.

Caring for the environment

Please help to keep the waterways pleasant places for everyone who uses them – and for the wildlife that depends on them.
- Shut gates behind you
- Keep to footpaths
- Don't light fires
- Respect the wildlife
- And take your litter away with you

Water discharge and oily bilges

Don't pump oily water from your bilge into the waterway. Well-maintained engines shouldn't leak oil, but check the drip tray under the engine and gearbox regularly. Use biodegradable oils, if possible. Avoid spilling petrol and diesel. If you do, mop it up – don't use detergents.

The toilets on your boat mustn't discharge sewage into the waterway. There are pump-out facilities for chemical or closed toilet systems at marinas and sanitary stations. Use the minimum amount of chemicals to avoid upsetting the sewage treatment system. If you have a closed toilet system, you may not need to use chemicals at all – so check your manual.

The wastewater outlet from your sink and shower is allowed to flow straight into the waterway. But to help keep the water as healthy as possible, put your cooking waste in the bin, use phosphate-free detergents and be economical with everything you put down the sink.

Report any pollution or fly-tipping to the Environment Agency pollution hotline on freephone 0800 80 70 60

Litter

Please don't throw any waste overboard – even apple cores take a long time to rot. Litter can kill wildlife, and it can cause problems for other boaters by getting tangled in their propellers. There are plenty of waste disposal points at marinas, moorings and along the waterway.

Wildlife

When you go too fast, your waves can damage banks and sensitive plants. If you see your wash hitting the bank, please slow down. Cut your speed and keep your distance when passing nesting water birds too.

The non-towpath side of the canal is often especially rich in wildlife, so take special care not to disturb plants or animals there. Don't moor on this side unless there are proper mooring facilities.

Respecting other waterway users

Waterways tend to be quiet, peaceful places. And they're for everyone to enjoy – boaters, walkers, anglers, cyclists and others.

Roaring engines, unnecessary use of the horn, loud music and shouting – they can all be a real nuisance to other people and wildlife.

Don't put your mooring stakes or ropes where people could trip over them. If you're passing an angler, keep to the centre of the channel unless they ask otherwise. Reduce your wash, but keep a steady pace.

Always slow down before passing other boats, whether they're moored up or travelling towards you.

Contacts

The **Environment Agency** is responsible for the River Thames, Anglian waterways and the River Medway. Local navigation information about each of these is available on 08708 506506 or at www.environment-agency.gov.uk/navigation
To report an incident to the Environment Agency, call 087 08 506 506.

British Waterways is responsible for the majority of the remaining canal and river navigations in England, Scotland and Wales. It has thirteen regional offices. Local navigation information, including maps showing the location of boater facilities, is contained in the Boaters Guide on www.waterscape.com/boating/guides.

To report an incident to British Waterways, go to www.britishwaterways.co.uk/responsibilities/safety. You can file your report online, or download a form and send it to us. Forms are also available from British Waterways Customer Service Centre on 01923 201120.
In an emergency, call 0800 47 999 47

Contacts for other navigation authorities are available from the **Association of Inland Navigation Authorities,** www.aina.org.uk or call 0113 243 3125 or email info@aina.org.uk

Maps and local guides
Inland Waterways of Great Britain – complete route planning and restoration map – Waterways World on 01283 742970

Nicholson's Ordnance Survey Inland Waterways Map of Great Britain – from good bookshops

Nicholson's Ordnance Survey Guides to the waterways – from good bookshops

GeoProjects Waterways Maps – 0118 939 3567 or email enquiries@geoprojects.demon.co.uk

Pearsons Canal Companions – 01283 713674

Inland Waterways Association Mail Order Service – www.iwashop.com or 01923 711114

Further Information

Further Information

Boat Safety Scheme: essential for all boat owners – boat construction standards and regular tests required by all licence-holders on British Waterways and Environment Agency waterways. The BSS is gradually being adopted by other authorities. Call 01923 201120 for details.

The Green Blue: practical advice and information on green products to help you save money and protect water quality and habitats. www.thegreenblue.org.uk A joint venture by the British Marine Federation and Royal Yachting Association.

EuroRegs for Inland Waterways: A pleasure boater's guide to CEVNI, Marian Martin, Royal Yachting Association. Essential information for anyone planning to cruise on tidal waterways.
Available from RYA call 023 8062 7462, fax 023 8062 7417 or email motor.boating@rya.org.uk

Other useful information
The RYA Book of Knots £7.99, available from RYA call +44 (0) 2380 604 100

Training

Boat-handling training courses:
We recommend that you take a professionally run course in boat handling, particularly if you are planning to boat regularly. The knowledge you gain will make your boating safer and more enjoyable. The RYA Certificate is effectively the waterways' driving licence. This is not compulsory in this country but is required in some places abroad.

Royal Yachting Association Inland Waters Helmsman's Certificate. One or two-day course. Call 023 8062 7462, fax 023 8062 7417 or email motor.boating@rya.org.uk for details of RYA recognised schools. The Practical Course Notes for this course are available to buy. Contact your local boat clubs too.

National Community Boats Association Certificate in Community Boat Management (CCBM). An intensive two-day course covering boat handling and the management of group safety and welfare. Call 02476 397400, fax 02476 392611 or email staff@national-cba.co.uk for details of NCBA boating courses. www.national-cba.co.uk

Printed in Great Britain
by Amazon